Native Americans

Ute

Barbara A. Gray-Kanatiiosh

ABDO Publishing Company

visit us at
www.abdopub.com

Published by ABDO Publishing Company, 4940 Viking Drive, Suite 622, Edina, Minnesota 55435. Copyright © 2004 by Abdo Consulting Group, Inc. International copyrights reserved in all countries. No part of this book may be reproduced in any form without written permission from the publisher.

Printed in the United States.

Cover Photo: Corbis
Interior Photos: AP/Wide World p. 28; Corbis pp. 4, 29, 30
Illustrations: David Kanietakeron Fadden pp. 7, 9, 11, 13, 15, 17, 19, 21, 23, 25, 27
Editors: Kate A. Conley, Jennifer R. Krueger, Kristin Van Cleaf
Art Direction & Maps: Neil Klinepier

Library of Congress Cataloging-in-Publication Data

Gray-Kanatiiosh, Barbara A., 1963-
    Ute / Barbara A. Gray-Kanatiiosh.
        p. cm. -- (Native Americans)
    Includes bibliographical references and index.
    Summary: An introduction to the history, social structure, customs, and present life of the Ute Indians.
      ISBN 1-57765-940-6
    1. Ute Indians--History--Juvenile literature. 2. Ute Indians--Social life and customs--Juvenile literature. [1. Ute Indians. 2. Indians of North America--Utah. 3. Indians of North America--Colorado. 4. Indians of North America--New Mexico.] I. Title. II. Native Americans (Edina, Minn.)

E99.U8G73 2003
979.004'9745--dc21

2003040338

About the Author: Barbara A. Gray-Kanatiiosh, JD
Barbara Gray-Kanatiiosh, JD, Ph.D. ABD, is an Akwesasne Mohawk. She resides at the Mohawk Nation and is of the Wolf Clan. She has a Juris Doctorate from Arizona State University, where she was one of the first recipients of ASU's special certificate in Indian Law. Barbara's Ph.D. is in Justice Studies at ASU. She is currently working on her dissertation, which concerns the impacts of environmental injustice on indigenous culture. Barbara works hard to educate children about Native Americans through her writing and Web site, where children may ask questions and receive a written response about the Haudenosaunee culture. The Web site is: www.peace4turtleisland.org

About the Illustrator: David Kanietakeron Fadden
David Kanietakeron Fadden is a member of the Akwesasne Mohawk Wolf Clan. His work has appeared in publications such as *Akwesasne Notes*, *Indian Time*, and the *Northeast Indian Quarterly*. Examples of his work have also appeared in various publications of the Six Nations Indian Museum in Onchiota, NY. His work has also appeared in "How the West Was Lost: Always the Enemy," produced by Gannett Production, which appeared on the Discovery Channel. David's work has been exhibited in Albany, NY; the Lake Placid Center for the Arts; Centre Strathearn in Montreal, Quebec; North Country Community College in Saranac Lake, NY; Paul Smith's College in Paul Smiths, NY; and at the Unison Arts & Learning Center in New Paltz, NY.

Contents

Where They Lived

The traditional Ute (YOOT) homelands were around the region of the Great Basin and the Colorado Plateau. Their territory included portions of present-day Colorado, Utah, northern New Mexico, and northeastern Arizona.

Centuries of **eroding** winds and rushing rivers carved a beautiful landscape. There were deserts, mountains, plateaus, and canyons. There were also meadows, marshes, and grasslands. The land held forests of ponderosa and lodgepole pine, piñon, juniper, and spruce trees. Dogwood, cottonwood, mesquite, and sagebrush grew at lower levels.

Chimney Rock on the Ute Mountain Indian Reservation near Cortez, Colorado

The Ute called themselves the Nuciu (NOO-chee-oh). Nuciu means "the people," or "high land people." The Ute spoke Shoshone, which belongs to the Numic branch of the Uto-Aztecan language family. The Ute's neighbors included the Arapaho, Comanche, Navajo, Paiute, and Shoshone tribes.

Ute Homelands

Society

The Ute society was divided into bands. These bands lived in different areas of Ute territory. The bands included the Mouache, Capote, Weeminuche, Tabequache, Grand River, White River, and the Uintah.

The people of each band chose a chief. The chief led not by force, but by earning the respect of his people. These band chiefs led the people in peace and war. Medicine people also cared for the band members. These people were skilled in using plants and ceremonies to heal.

In the spring, the Ute bands broke into smaller family units. This was necessary for the Ute to survive. The smaller units made traveling easier, which in turn made finding food easier. They followed **migrating** animals and gathered wild berries and vegetables as they ripened.

In the winter, the Ute came back together again. At this time, the Ute would socialize and participate in large festivals. Winter was also the time for arranging marriages and holding reunions.

Ute perform the bear dance.

Food

Ute men went hunting to find food. They used spears, bows and arrows, and snares. The men hunted many different animals. They hunted large animals such as elks, pronghorn, bison, and deer. They also hunted smaller animals such as squirrels and rabbits. In addition, the men hunted birds such as ducks, geese, quail, doves, and grouse.

The Ute fished using a hook and line. They also used spears carved from wood. The spears had barbs, or sharp points, at the end. These barbs prevented the fish from flopping off the spear. The Ute fished for trout, bass, and other panfish.

But, the Ute did not get all of their food from hunting and fishing. They also gathered barks, wild roots, wild vegetables, and medicinal plants. The Ute rarely planted gardens, however. When they did, they planted corn, beans, and squashes. They ground the corn into flour and used it to make bread and mush.

The Ute ate their food in season, but they also preserved some food for the winter. The Ute sometimes dried their meat and fish. They mixed the dried meats with wild berries and buffalo fat to make pemmican (PEH-mih-kuhn).

A Ute man gathers plants and wild roots.

Homes

For many years, the Ute lived in brush shelters. Each one held about 12 people. The Ute covered the frames of these shelters with brush. Sometimes they used handwoven reed or grass mats to cover the shelters. They tied these mats onto the wooden frame with willow strips.

The Ute began living in tepees after they were introduced to horses. Tepees were easier to move than brush shelters. That's because horses could carry the tepees from camp to camp as the Ute hunted.

The Ute made tepees with long wooden poles. Women set up the poles to form a cone. The women then stretched a cover over the frame.

A tepee cover was made from the hides of American bison, which are also known as buffalo. Women sewed about 15 buffalo hides together to make one tepee cover. The covers were painted with **geometric** designs or **pictographs**.

Wooden stakes pinned the tepee cover to the ground. Long wooden pins held the two ends of the cover together. Below the pins, the Ute left an opening for the door. They also left a smoke hole at the top. Inside, the Ute slept on reed mats and furs around a fire.

A Ute tepee and brush shelter

Clothing

The Ute made and decorated their clothing with the plants and animals they found in their environment. What they did not eat, they used for clothing, decoration, or tools. There was no waste. They traded extra food and clothing with neighboring tribes.

The Ute made their clothing from deer, elk, and buffalo skins. They sewed with thread made from animal **sinew**. Needles were carved from bone. They used antler, bone, and stone **awls** to punch holes in hides.

Men wore fringed leather shirts, **breechcloths**, and moccasins. They also wore leather leggings or pants. The leggings had long fringes along the outside seam. Leggings protected their legs from sharp thorns and brush. Sometimes, the Ute painted or quilled the fringes that were on their shirts and leggings.

Women wore fringed leather dresses. The dresses were long and decorated with elk teeth, bear claws, or round shell beads.

Ute women wore wide belts. They also wore fringed leggings under their dresses. They wrapped the legging around the leg between the knee and the top of the moccasin.

The Ute also had other types of clothes. In colder weather, for example, the Ute wore fur robes. They also wore special clothing for ceremonies. The Ute decorated ceremonial clothing with porcupine quillwork and beadwork. They painted their clothing with **geometric** designs and **pictographs**.

Ute clothing

Crafts

The Ute were skilled **artisans**. One skill was making baskets. Women crafted **utility**, medicine, and wedding baskets from reeds and willow. They used natural dyes to color the basket materials red, black, or yellow.

Women decorated clothing with porcupine quills and glass beads. They dyed some of the porcupine quills for this purpose. Quills were hard when dry. So, women wet the quills to soften them and quickly sewed them onto clothing. They made beautiful **geometric** and floral designs with the quills.

Today, Ute women commonly use glass beads instead of quills. Glass beads were introduced by European traders. The Ute decorate **cradleboard** covers, vests, leggings, collars, **pendants**, moccasins, rattle handles, and **gauntlets** with beads.

Women use two types of beading stitches. One is called the peyote stitch, and the other is called the lazy stitch. The peyote stitch is used on rattle handles. The lazy stitch is used for beading on clothing. The lazy stitch can be used to bead floral, **geometric**, and animal designs.

Ute women weave baskets with natural materials.

Family

Ute families were close. An extended family of aunts, uncles, cousins, and grandparents lived together in a camp. Every family member was important to the survival of the band. Each person contributed by helping with daily chores.

Men hunted for food and protected the families. They made the tools and weapons they needed for hunting and fishing. They made these tools from bone, flint, and antler. Men also made knives and stone axes. They used the axes to harvest trees they would later use for their tepees.

Women were responsible for the home, food, and clothing. Women used digging sticks to harvest wild onions and other edible roots. They also gathered berries and medicinal plants in woven baskets. Women were also responsible for drying food for the winter.

Like the men and the women, the elders of the band also had special responsibilities. They helped by showing young ones how to weave and make tools and weapons. They also told the history of the Ute and taught the children by telling stories.

A Ute elder tells a story.

Children

The Ute loved their children and taught them important skills. Children learned by watching and helping the family with daily chores. Girls watched as the older women made **cradleboards**. From watching the older women, Ute girls learned how to make their own cradleboards.

A cradleboard was made from willow. Its oval frame was wide at the top, and it narrowed toward the bottom. At the top of the board, a protective willow band kept the baby's head safe. The baby was placed inside a leather pouch that covered the board. An older girl might carry a baby in a cradleboard on her back.

Girls also helped the women prepare hides for clothing. They helped remove the meat and hair from the hides by using scrapes. Next, the Ute tanned and stretched the hides. Then, the leather was ready to be made into clothing.

Ute boys also learned a lot from watching the men in their band. Boys learned how to hunt and fish. They hunted rabbits and other small game with bows and arrows. Older boys learned how to identify animal tracks and quietly follow them.

However, the children did not spend all their time watching the adults. They also played games. One game was played with a **vertebra** of a bird. The children attached a short cord to the vertebra. At the other end of the cord was a small wooden pin. The object of the game was to catch the vertebra on the wooden pin.

This Ute child learns from an elder how to make cradleboards.

Myths

During the winter, the Ute would tell stories around the campfire. They still share these stories today during gatherings. One of these stories recounts how the earth was created.

A long time ago, the world we know today did not exist. In the Sky World sat the Creator. He was all alone.

The Creator opened a hole in the Sky World. He picked up a giant broom and began to sweep pebbles, dust, and dirt through the hole. The Creator looked down and was delighted to see that the dust, dirt, and pebbles turned into mountains, plateaus, and rolling hills. This became the earth.

The Creator poured water and ice through the Sky Hole. This became rain and snow. They made everything look pretty. In the moist soil, the Creator planted trees, flowers, and other plants.

The Creator picked up fallen leaves and threw them into the air. The leaves became birds with beautiful songs and colors. Then, he created the Ute. He created animals and fish. He taught the Ute how to do ceremonies and how to hunt and fish.

The Creator throws
leaves into the air.

21

War

Before meeting Europeans, war was rare among the Ute. But, sometimes the Ute fought in small battles when neighboring tribes invaded their lands. The Ute depended on the land for survival. So, sometimes these wars were necessary to protect Ute hunting, fishing, and gathering territory.

In war, the Ute used bows and arrows for distant fighting. In close fighting, they used knives with blades made of quartz, a clear, hard mineral. Or, they used their fists. The Ute often painted their faces and clothes before going into battle.

The Ute wore breastplates made from bone beads. They also wore wide bone-bead chokers around their necks. Breastplates and chokers were worn like armor. The bone beads protected the wearer's neck and chest from arrows.

Horses were also an important part of how the Ute fought in wars. The Ute were skilled horsemen. Neighboring tribes also had horses. Horses allowed the Ute and neighboring tribes to cross more easily into each other's lands.

Raiding became common. Sometimes the Ute did not kill the enemy. Instead, they counted coup. Counting coup is riding into the enemy's camp and touching the enemy with a stick. This was a great show of bravery for the Ute, and no one died.

This Ute man protects himself in battle with a choker and breastplates made from bone beads.

Contact with Europeans

In the 1600s, the Ute traded with Spaniards who lived in New Mexico. Horses were one of the items that the Ute traded with the Spaniards. This is how the Ute became one of the first native peoples to have horses.

However, not all contact with Europeans was positive. Around the 1850s, miners found gold and copper in Ute territory. Settlers flooded into the area in hopes of striking it rich. The settlers wanted the Ute's lands. The U.S. military was sent in to protect the settlers and miners. The Ute fought back.

The Ute also had no **immunity** to European illnesses. Many died from **measles epidemics**. Soon, the Ute were forced to sign treaties and give up large areas of land. They were relocated to reservations.

Once on reservations, the U.S. government wanted the Ute to give up some of their ways. It wanted the Ute people to settle in one place and be farmers. The U.S. government even outlawed Ute ceremonies such as the sun dance.

24

In the early 1800s, both Spanish and
Mexican traders journeyed into Ute lands.

Ouray

Ouray (OO-ray) was a famous Ute chief. He was born in 1833. Ouray grew up in a time of great conflict for the Ute. Both settlers and the U.S. government wanted Ute lands. The Ute had to fight to protect their lands and way of life.

Ouray saw the war and bloodshed. He saw how neighboring tribes were being mistreated, and he did not want his people to suffer. Ouray became the leader who led the Ute through this difficult time.

Ouray believed the best way to prevent bloodshed was to arrange treaties with the U.S. government. Because he spoke several languages, including English, it was easier for him to arrange these peace treaties. Ouray even met with President Ulysses Grant in an attempt to protect the Ute and their culture.

Ouray did what he could to protect his people and his land. He tried his best to negotiate respectfully with the new settlers. However, the Ute were eventually confined to a reservation set aside for them by the U.S. government. Ouray died in 1880.

Chief Ouray

27

The Ute Today

Today, the Ute live on three **federally recognized** reservations. They are located in Colorado and Utah. In the year 2000, there were about 7,000 Ute.

One of these reservations is the Unintah & Ouray Reservation, located in Utah. Another is the Southern Ute Reservation, located near Ignacio, Colorado. The Ute also have a reservation called the Ute Mountain Reservation near Towaoc, Colorado.

The Ute **economy** has changed much in the Ute's long history. Today, a large percentage of their income is earned from the sale of natural resources such as timber, gas, and oil. One of the Ute reservations even has a pottery plant.

A Ute dancer performs at the welcoming ceremony for the 2002 Olympics.

28

The Ute are working to preserve their culture. Annual dances such as the bear and sun dance are the foundation of Ute traditions. Sun dances are sacred and held in the summer. The bear dance is held in springtime and lasts for several days. During the dance there is also singing, eating, and prayer offerings.

The Ute also continue to make their traditional crafts. For example, the women create beautiful beaded works of art. They bead purses, vests, ties, moccasins, and other clothing as they preserve their traditional skills through art.

A Ute Native American dances during a powwow of the Ute National Council.

A tepee in a Ute Indian museum in Montrose, Colorado

Glossary

artisan - a person skilled in a craft or trade.

awl - a pointed tool for making small holes in materials, such as leather or wood.

breechcloth - a piece of hide or cloth, usually worn by men, that wraps between the legs and ties with a belt around the waist.

cradleboard - a flat board used to hold a baby. It could be carried on the mother's back or hung from a tree so that the baby could see what was going on.

economy - the way a tribe uses its money, goods, and natural resources.

epidemic - the rapid spread of a disease among many people.

erode - to wash or wear away.

federal recognition - the U.S. government's recognition of a tribe as being an independent nation. The tribe is then eligible for special funding and for protection of its reservation lands.

gauntlet - a heavy glove.

geometric - made up of straight lines, circles, and other simple shapes.

immunity - protection against disease.

measles - an illness that causes a fever and rash.

migrate - to move from one place to settle in another.

pendant - a hanging ornament.

pictograph - a picture that represents a word or idea.

sinew - a band of tough fibers that joins a muscle to a bone.

utility - made to be used in a practical way.

vertebra - one of the bones that makes up the backbone.

Web Sites

To learn more about the Ute, visit ABDO Publishing Company on the World Wide Web at **www.abdopub.com**. Web sites about the Ute are featured on our Book Links page. These links are routinely monitored and updated to provide the most current information available.

Index